THE SMELL OF ABSENCE

MICHAEL IMOSSAN

To the women who planted flowers in my body

This is a work of fiction. All names, characters, places, and incidents are a product of the author's imagination. Any resemblance to real events or persons, living or dead, is entirely coincidental.

Published by Akashic Books

ISBN: 978-1-63614-253-1

Printed in China
First printing

EU Authorized Representative details:
Easy Access System Europe
Mustamäe tee 50, 10621 Tallinn, Estonia
gpsr.request@easproject.com

Akashic Books
Instagram, X, Facebook: AkashicBooks
info@akashicbooks.com
www.akashicbooks.com

African Poetry Book Fund
Brown University
10 Prospect Street
Box A
Providence, RI 02912

TABLE OF CONTENTS

PREFACE

by Patricia Jabbeh Wesley

Michael Imossan's *The Smell of Absence* is a bitingly powerful, haunting collection of poems that explores pain and redemption. Imossan is part of a generation of Nigerian poets who are forging an exciting vision for the future through their intimate and piercing poetry. Line by line, each poem travels on a journey of father and son, absence and loss. This is a story about lost fathers, fathers who abandon themselves in abandoning their sons, and sons who find strength in the face of abandonment. Here are poems about a man revisiting his childhood through a speaker who can take empty spaces and turn them into vivid pictures of our lost youth. When it seems like we are reading about a boy experiencing loss, we meet ourselves. *The Smell of Absence* journeys into the void, uncovering hidden truths about how to meet the lost father, redeem oneself, and in redeeming oneself, redeem the father.

The chapbook opens with an autobiographical poem, "How I choose to begin the story." Imossan introduces himself as a young child being prepared for school. His first lesson of the day does not come from school, but from his mother:

> I follow her hands as she straightens my uniform,
> cups my face in her palms, and says,
> *you look like your father.*
> There's a garden burning in the honey of her eyes.
> I am both wound and scar—proof
> of my father cutting through her flowered dream.
> If time heals all wounds, what will it do to me?
> She tucks my shirt in, pats me on the back,
> says, *do not be like him.*

At the end of this advice is silence: absence not just of the father, but also of words. Imossan's audacity of language allows us to carry the words in our hands. In every poem, he gives himself the authority to present what he finds not just through sight, but also through smell.

The Smell of Absence reminds us that poetry is the most powerful tool we have to express our deepest emotions. The chapbook's journey begins with the speaker's birth mother, the true symbol of motherhood, then moves to the father, who is absent even while physically present, then to the stepmother. The juxtaposing of these relationships between child and parent, circling back to the father who is supposed to be present, is powerfully achieved.

From the experience of homelessness Imossan's speaker recalls from childhood—"I can still feel the rain / falling through our new roof" ("We ate through the thunder.")—to his return to the father/son relationship at the end of the collection, Imossan offers a new understanding of regret, pain, forgiveness, love, and finally, redemption. He writes:

> Close to the window, a piano
> cold from neglect leans
> against the wall. I walk to it,
> a dust-covered tune awaits
> my ears. I press my finger
> on a key and it resembles a tooth
> knocked backward
> into the mouth. The sound
> spilling from every corner becomes
> blood in my hands.
> *I am sorry, I didn't mean*
> *to hurt you,* I say.
>
> ("I fear I may hurt everything I touch.")

The Smell of Absence is not just the recollections of a boyhood enmeshed in loss—loss of home, father, and everything a child needs to survive—but also a story shared across Africa and the world. An urgently necessary story.

HOW I CHOOSE TO BEGIN THE STORY.

I begin this story with "I"
because it is more about me than the scar sutured
to the center of my dream,
more about me than the sky pouring
its blue self on our roof, slithering through
the flare-rusted zinc into our home.
It is Monday morning and she is dressing me
for school. From the broken table,
a documentary comes on the old gray
television. I do not watch it; instead,
I follow her hands as she straightens my uniform,
cups my face in her palms, and says,
you look like your father.
There's a garden burning in the honey of her eyes.
I am both wound and scar—proof
of my father cutting through her flowered dream.
If time heals all wounds, what will it do to me?
She tucks my shirt in, pats me on the back,
says, *do not be like him.*
The fan strapped to the ceiling, fatigued,
whistles an old tune.
I do not understand, but I hold her words
in my hands. And, like salt, I sprinkle them
along the stairs where I will step into my future.

WHERE THE ACHE SETTLES.

"Like any fatherless ache, the origin of my
displacement is untraceable."—Samuel Adeyemi

Noon. And my spine is
beginning to wrinkle. I strut through the day.
The sun, a golden pebble trapped
in the beads of sweat staggering along my brow.
A bucket of popcorn settled on my head.
I say to strangers: buy this popcorn
and rescue me from lack.
The open mouth of the street is my home.
The night, full of teeth, is where I will rest my head.
I can recite despair like a poem, like a widow
who, after her husband's death, sits beside his grave
singing the history of loss.
Saying to every passerby: you do not know
what death does to the house it passes through.
Come, sit with me and listen to the many ways
a heart can be wrecked. To tell you the truth,
I know where the sharp thing entered me,
so when I say my ache is fatherless, it is not
in the way Samuel said it.
What I mean is, I enter every day
thinking there's a wisp of light waiting to hug me.

WHAT IT MEANS TO BE A BASTARD.

What if I told you I
slept in my mother's skin
just to know what loneliness feels like?
What if I told you a pot of okra soup
boiling like a country on fire is
another name for survival?
What if I told you the tongue lifting
to meet the hard palate is how it
claims the word *love* for itself, and I
could never claim that word,
not in the way our neighbour's son
claimed it—riding his new bicycle across
Christmas. The wheels circling like a year
trying to hold itself by the hand.
Yes, I did what I did when the boy allowed
everyone to ride his bicycle except me.
I pressed my teeth into the day and ran toward
my mother because that's what fatherless boys do.
Don't look at me like that, what would you
have done if you were in my shoes?
I did not have a shoe, I walked barefoot
to school, my heels scraped clean
by the summer-heated tar.

NO LIGHT AT THE END OF THIS STORY, ONLY A QUESTION.

You came back for me somber, with regret on your lips,
whiskey on your breath, and a woman by your side.

I did not know what to say.
A man leaves his unborn child
and runs toward the dark. Leaves the mother
with her tummy protruding until loneliness
calcifies, becomes a shelter, a roof
above their heads. The story will always be
sad whatever version I tell:
the one where you leave or the one where you
return. And each time, I want
to have the music so loud it bleaches the pain.

I was nine when you came back.
Not for my mother but for me. You cut yourself
open and I saw my face running in your blood.
You said: see, blood does not flow the way of water.
Blood will always come back for blood. The air lifted
the smudge of white softness off my eyes,
and I saw both of us—the air and I—curled
over a question mark, like this—see?

ON THE NIGHT THE MOON SANK.

On my way to school, inside my now father's car, he turned to me and said: son, a man is a pocket full of mistakes. His breath clear as water. I do not know why I am telling you this. Maybe because the windshields were all up and the AC spat a florid winter through lavender-freshened vents or because I held his voice in my palm and it felt like regret, felt like a man kneeling inside his own wound. At the end of school, I came out to see his Benz squatting by the gate. The sun tiptoeing over its black paint. I should have gone home to my mom; instead, I followed him to his car. I do not know why. Perhaps it was summer and all I wanted was to feel the winter air crisp over my skin. Perhaps I wanted my own bicycle so badly I would follow any man that claimed me as his own—or perhaps he did not smell of whiskey, and I wanted to feel his sky-blue love tucked neatly into my uniform. We drove to an eatery where we had fried rice that tasted like two lovers licking themselves clean of love. The chicken, a roasted harmattan. When he dropped me off, the sky had darkened, the swallows had begun gifting their wings to the night air. My mother, with face the color of seawater, tore into two. *Where have you been? Where was that man when I lugged you on my shoulders searching for a roof to cover our shame?* she asked between sobs. I did not know what to say. I dropped my schoolbag and began crying with her—the moon sinking inside our tears.

WE ATE THROUGH THE THUNDER.

That morning is still caged in my heart—when the door
shivered to a knock. When
the landlord, with anger-stained face,
sculpted into a black shirt,
edged along the doorway. It was
thunder outside and I was too young to understand,
but I could see it on your face,
the sadness ripening like a new day.
Forgive me, there's so much story
trapped in my teeth. I slept
in a bed yesterday and the sky was still a sky—
satin blue spilled on white canvas.
I wanted a roof with nothing
attached to it so I walked inside dawn.
I have known to touch the world
like something with fangs. Forgive me,
I know you'd want me to forget.
Forgive me, I keep saying *forgive me.*
It was all you said to the landlord
before he flung us out in the rain,
our backs pressed against the cold
mouth of God. *I am sorry*, you said
to me as if it were your fault, as if our home
-lessness was a gun you held against my face.
The world moved past us. We ate
through the thunder to be here.
But where is *here?* I can still feel the rain
falling through our new roof.

SEARCHING FOR WHO TO CLAIM ME.

Though I am far from the place of my birth,
the girl playing a piano by the sidewalk
is leading me into the past, she is writing constellations in songs,
she is saying: a note, too, can be a map to self-discovery.
And I am searching for myself in songs,
reinventing the logic of philosophy, of cartographers
who drew maps on their skin and said, I must know what poetry
lives inside me, I must know what music will stir
these fingers into surrender.
I follow her tune to where a woman lifts a boy
to the heavens, saying: this boy, though born out of wedlock,
though christened unwanted, I shall keep him.
I watch as the regret in her eyes congeals into scars.
I watch as despair gathers like water,
like the sea gathering itself into the namelessness of waves.
I do not wait to watch them pour, to watch as tears
perform the duty of baptism. I follow the tune to where
a boy with dagger-edged questions, with a purple blade
tongue asks me, who is your father? Do you not have
better shoes? I want to tell him I know nothing
of possession, that my shoes, having walked upon emptiness,
have had their souls broken by thirst.
But the sun leans into my mouth. I chop my sentences
into sounds, humming the tune toward a road that leads to nowhere,
searching for who to claim me, searching—

TABOO.

Not that I hate the church,
but if this will suffice, the church hated me first.

I, a taboo, what do I know of the priest's
voice summoning God into my infant life?

What do I know of baptism other than the
liquid eyes of my mother dripping over me?

It is a Sunday morning
and feet are hurrying toward holiness, toward doors
that open into God.
I and my mother have walked through
that door. Close to the podium, grace falls
from the choristers' mouths. Their voices calling
everyone to the duty of worship.

The walls of this church have known
my mother's nakedness. One time, she knelt
in the auditorium, stripping bare her shame before the priest,
pleading baptism for me, begging to be answered by water,
her bougainvillea gown sprawled over the floor.

No sympathy was offered her.
Only the long monochrome of rejection.
Only the lustrous spectacle of hate. Amen.

WHAT GUILT DID TO ME.

Maybe I wanted to belong to someone, a man,
so I parked my bags and left. I was nine, his car waiting

by the side of Christmas. Your face, a stick wrapped
in sulfur, waiting to spark. The sky, a parade of fireworks.

The promise of a bicycle blooming inside me.
You did not move, you stood still like something nailed

to the ground, your eyes following me to the door of his
black Benz. Through the harmattan-stained glass, I watched

you become a silhouette, the road lengthening you
into a memory, into an ellipsis. This is how innocence

can be guilty; your voice, a sad song through the telephone
and my lips pressed against silence as you kept repeating

my name, *Michael, Michael.* I did not know that you had thrown
yourself away just so you could be light enough to carry

me through the years, my four-year-old self strapped to your
back. That opening and closing the night for strangers

was how you fed me into bloom. Isn't this why my mouth is full
of *forgive me?* Why, after I knew what I knew, I knelt

inside my shame and muttered *forgive me.* I swear at age 13, after
my stepmother had starved me for three days, I wanted to come back

but I did not know how, I did not know you were waiting for me
to return home—arms flung open like a wind-beaten door.

NOT ALL BLOOD IS THICKER THAN WATER.

From the distance, my father's car blossomed into view.
Behind him, the day kept falling as if something
had pushed it off the horizon. Where does everyone
go after the music fades? After the lights have
been turned off—our sinew trampled, knee-deep
in the mud of time. The halls are emptying
themselves of music and I am a lone lamb grinding
to this thin emptiness. Everyone has left, their feet shuffled
against *we-do-not-want-you.* Their backs turned
to my outstretched hands. I wish you were here to see it.
How three months after staying with my father,
I picked up a razor blade and edged a door into my wrist.
Look, the opening still bright as a wet mouth. How one night,
after reading Amma Darko's *Faceless,*
I flowed into the street, slept in its wide gutters until
the sky found me. I have knocked on wrong
doors only to watch them open. This is what
I learned: water is a language spoken by the body
when in awe of its own breaking. And I have been smashed
against several todays, my body broken into bits of black hums.
His car rolled into the compound. The gates were flung wide.
Night spilled into every corner. The birds sliced
the air open like what prayer does to the lips it falls
out of. I did not move, I stood like something carved
out of rebellion. My stepsiblings ran toward him, their lips spiced
with *daddy welcome,* their hands lifting happiness in large
bags from the backseat of the car—but it wasn't rebellion,
it was my legs heavy with the memory of you; the day you
came back from work holding a bag of apples in your hands.

I did not move, I stood there, feet stamped to the ground,
sculpting the night into the shape of your smile.

WHAT IT MEANS TO STEP INTO SUNRISE.

Another morning of legs stealing
into my room, his wife far from the hush of his
tone. It was five a.m. and the crickets kept calling
us into their songs. I could feel the fear
running through him but I did not know why,
I did not know that to love a woman
that did not love your son was to walk on a broken
poem, sharp oxymorons spilled on the floor.
This is the weight of love carried into the day.
This is a story forced out of a new dawn,
an entire house coming down on a thirteen-year-old boy.
I let him kiss me on the forehead, the wet
of his lips melding to my skin. I cannot recall
but I think he said *I love you* before squeezing some
naira notes into my palm.
The room was dark, but our voices, lit like a burning
house, brightened its walls. I saw his eyes, two
lilies carved out of a dying garden.
When he told me he was leaving for three weeks,
my body woke up in fear. I thought
of stepmother's whip landing on my back, I thought
of dawn opening into a funeral house, my laughter
dressed in black. I thought of the curses, the way
my stepmother, twirling in a storm of disgust,
would force me open like a jammed door.
And after his car drove away,
I packed my legs, followed the back door and ran
into the unfurling light. My eyes a pool of sunrise.

I HOPE THE DAY BREAKS BEFORE I DO.

The boy begging at the market has holes all
over his body.
                    Every language begins with the throat
                    opening. Every word is a hand stretching
toward desire. Have I not told you what I passed
through to be here: the cracking of heat on
                    my bare back, sweat pooling around my
                    shoulders as I lifted the burdens of strangers
to the trunks of their cars. The way I vomited
a truckload of *thank yous* when they handed
                    me some change. It is the way fatherless
                    boys survive the storm of living. Have I not
pointed you to the boy begging at the market?
Look closer and you'll see my face in his face.
                    My throat opening toward the word *hunger*.
                    I swear I did not follow the man home because
I believed he was my father, but because I saw a door in his hands.

It is night and the sky is beginning to close its eyes.
                    The stalls will run into darkness. Like a ditch,
every stranger will jump over this boy and he will be left
to wander in his hunger, hoping the day breaks
before he does.

FEMININE LIGHT.

If not my mother, then my aunty.
If not my aunty, then the lights passing

through this July glass. I am tired
of calling myself bastard in poems. Here is

my father wrapped in whiskey and honeycomb
apology. Here is a decade-old story locked

in my throat. Here is the woman by his side,
crackling like red oil steeped in fire. Yes,

there is a name affixed to my suffering.
It is called stepmother. Her story goes:

I wanted a father so much so I claimed one.
I wanted a beautiful home so I ran inside

someone's house. Once, I wrapped my hands
around my body just to know what it felt

like to be hugged by a man. See? I am happy now,
my lips stretched into a pink dash. A knife

passing through the body only teaches it healing
and there is a scar on my left wrist the size

of a lesson. Forget all I have said, I have drunk two
decades' worth of water, still there is a thirst

festering inside me. Think of it this way,
I wasn't fatherless, I was only filled with too

much feminine light.

WISHING A STAR WOULD GROW FROM MY WOUND.

No, it was never
about the house and how it grew smaller
in his absence, never about my stepsiblings
and how they carried him on their lips
in the way I could never carry him.
It was about the night. How it knew
every morning that slithered through
my window was already broken.
My room was empty save for the foam
where I soaked myself.
There were cracks on its walls
where, in the dark, a loud silence crawled out.
Once, I stood before it and heard a song,
the way it weakened my knees like a child
caught by trembling.
There's a pain for boys whose fathers do not belong
to them. Once, I stood in the center
of it, hoping joy would startle me. Nothing happened.
Only the silence. Crisp, frightening silence.

THE SMELL OF ABSENCE.

As if the day,
already gone,
was a road that led to you.
I walked through it,
walked through the hostel field.
Everywhere was calm.
The sky was beginning to fall asleep.
The swallows sought shelter
in nearby trees.
The grass, wet with the softness of evening dew
knew the weight of my feet,
knew my body was a city full
of abandoned houses.
There's nothing worth gifting here.
The sadness of a boy belongs to the boy
just like your loneliness belonged to you.
Just like I bumped into your crying
and found father's watery silhouette edged
along your cheeks.
The visiting day had long gone—
still, I carried in my eyes the sight of mothers
pouring into their children.
Your absence, a fragrance so strong it followed
me around.

MOTHER FORGIVE ME, FOR I HAVE SINNED.

Surprisingly,
I began to forget you,
the image of your hands pressing
down a salmon, silver steel gliding
in and out of it.
I began to forget the shape of your face.
Memory wiped clean like blue
ink on white board. I forgot
my father's house, forgot the sting
of stepmother's whip. My siblings
and how they often looked at me
like something salvaged from a dumpster.
I followed *the boys*. We were all equals here.
There's something about the absence
of love that makes a thing go wild.
The wolf knows this story better.
I followed *the boys* to the place where
a girl's skirt lifted above her waist
was how to become a man.
They handed me the condom.
Mother, I am sorry. Forgive me, for I
have sinned. I was only fourteen
and wanted to become a man so badly.

LAYING A STEM TO REST.

Softness is what we
beg of the earth when the drought
lingers for too long.
My aunty and I tilled the soil to lay cassava
stems inside, hoping they'd grow wings.
Not too far from us, another farm.
I could see a young boy run through it,
a thread tied to a kite unspooled
behind him. I was not that boy.
Now, I am standing before
the gravediggers, begging softness
out of the earth.
I hold your body for the last time
before letting go, before laying
it into the ground. I shovel the sands
back. I water the closing with my tears.

MY FORGIVENESS IS A BLOOMING LILY.

Now, the years having s t r e t c h e d
me into an animal full of understanding, I know
what guilt does to a man—
the way my father, wanting to apologize, opened
the door to my room. How he stood there
looking at me like something remembered.
I wanted to forgive him. I saw the way his eyes
glistened with remorse.
How he pressed his knees against the faded tile
of my floor like something conquered and began weeping.
I did not weep with him, but I felt his sobbing.
I ran inside his open arms not because I wanted him
to call me *son* but because I wanted him to stay,
because I knew there was a woman that wasn't my mother
waking the night up in search for him.
The way he kept crying as if there was salvation
in his sobs. The absence was still there,
loud as a gunshot, loud as a mother's grief.
I could feel it in the stench of the whiskey that swelled
over him. Father, I am twenty-five now. The years have grown
larger than my grudge. November twinkles over
the emptiness of my bed like a little star. I do not drink.
I have tried keeping my hands from touching any girl
I do not want to walk into forever with. Yet
the woman at the bus station says I look like you,
says I look like a man flipping through the years in search
of what he'd lost.
I am standing in front of the mirror now,
wiping you off my reflection like tears. I can see

your face growing out of mine, how the s
in *sorry* presses against the mouth's white marble
before opening it into an apology. Here is my forgiveness,
white as a blooming lily.

I FEAR I MAY HURT EVERYTHING I TOUCH.

Twenty-seven years
and I am all by myself.
            My room,
a skin ironed by solitude,
            is all that wraps
its hands around me.
Remember the woman
at the bus station who said I
looked like my father?
It's been two years now,
still, fear sharpens my body
like a knife.
Every woman I touch looks
like my mother's tears. I do not plan
on running into the dark,
on wearing disappearance
as a skin, but I am scared my father's
legs belong to me, I am scared
his hands are my hands and
everything I approach may
hurt from my touch.
Close to the window, a piano
cold from neglect leans
against the wall. I walk to it,
a dust-covered tune awaits
my ears. I press my finger
on a key and it resembles a tooth
knocked backward
into the mouth. The sound

spilling from every corner becomes
blood in my hands.
I am sorry, I didn't mean
to hurt you, I say.

ACKNOWLEDGMENTS

I sincerely acknowledge the magazines in which the following poems were published in earlier forms:

Ake Review: "No light at the end of this story, only a question" and "Searching for who to claim me"

Full House: "How I choose to begin the story"